Ask Me Another Way

Poems and Poetry
by Steven Sassmann

Kansas City   Misssouri

Spartan Press
Kansas City, MO
spartanpresskc.com

Copyright ©Steven Sassmann, 2019
First Edition 1 3 5 7 9 10 8 6 4 2
ISBN: 978-1-950380-43-5
LCCN: 2019943283

Design, edits and layout: Steven Sassmann
Cover image: *Le Printemps* by William Adolphe Bouguereau
Title page image: Steven Sassmann
Author photo: Mary Sassmann
All rights reserved. No part of this publication may be reproduced or transmitted in any form or by any means, electronic or mechanical, including photocopying, recording or by info retrieval system, without prior written permission from the author.

The Author wishes to thank the many people who have influenced his Poetry; mostly the Readers and the Writers. And to Thank the Publishers and Editors who have chosen his work for inclusion in their Books, Anthologies, and Magazines - both paper and electronic, and for choosing his Poems as contest winners. The author also wishes to acknowledge a few great Teachers for their encouragement given him at crucial times in his life. And Sincere Thanks to the Teachers who have used my Poems and Essays in their classrooms and have translated my work into other languages.

You have always been taught that these statements must be made in the 3rd person. You found that writing in the third person is a good way to mine the hidden veins of thought. But in learning to think for YourSelf, You have come to believe that, in some cases, writing of yourself in 3rd person is an artificial affectation.

So as the Author, I wish to Sincerely Thank the people who have kindly helped me to become who I am; and if I'm Lucky in the future, as the Poet You won't truly see until after I'm gone.

Thank You Mary & Brian & Joyce, and Robert & Marcella and Michael, Shon & Rusty. Thank You Apryl & Alicia, Melvin & Roy & Jared & April, Georgia, Wendy, Armeli, Iulia & Raul & Felix, Duong, Adrienne, Elleraine, and Tony & Kyle & Todd. Thank You Boris, Owen, Christine, Rajdeep, Catherine, Adhikari, Valerie, and of course my #1 fan, Victoria. Thank You Mike & Ad Astra, and Lori & Jason. Thank You to Teachers: Alice.H & George.Mc & Rick.B & Paul.B and Estelle from Hell. And Special Thanks to Terri & Art.

Look what they've done to my song. - Melanie Safka

TABLE OF CONTENTS

While You're Waiting / 1
Art Is / 2
Verb / 3
FlowerChild / 4
Imagine Being Sane / 5
Me And Robert And God / 6
So Show Me Your Kitty / 7
That Look / 8
Home Run / 9
Object Of Art / 10
Tonya / 11
Unlimited Potential / 12
 Summer Solstice / 13
Now I Know / 14
Sex On TV / 15
She Can't Help It / 16
F Like Crazy / 17
DrumBeat / 18
Once Were Stars / 19
I Was Too Busy / 20
Eight Billion / 21
God Speaks / 22
Stars Speak / 23
We'll Be Rain / 24
Creator-Destroyer / 25
Never Look / 26
If By If / 27
Words / 28
The Box / 29

The Real World / 30
Ain't That / 31
Fukushima Fish / 32
The American Dream / 33
Red Reminder / 34
First Steps / 35
American Medicine / 36
Perfect Flaw / 37
Don't Believe In Science / 38
Tricky Little Things / 39
This Changed Everything / 40
Living In The Past / 41
Truth Was Not Enough / 42
Silence Is Magnetic / 43
El Norte / 44
Price Of Heart / 45
Impossible / 46
MoneyBurn / 47
Hypnosis / 48
Someday / 49
Nothing / 50
Ocean Witch / 51
Right Where They Live / 52
No Way Out / 53
The Economy / 54
Always Be Comedy / 55
Only / 56
Sky Blue Mind / 57
Color Of Sun / 58
Noblesse Oblige / 59

Turn It Off / 60
Educatin' Michelangelo / 61
All Became The Same / 62
Heavenly Body / 63
Delphi / 64
We See Better / 65
Nobody Could Prove Anything / 66
Poems And Poetry / 67
It Stops It / 68
I Believe / 69
Spherical Vagina / 70
Our Government / 71
They Miss / 72
Distillation / 73
Good Poem Good Sex / 74
It Belongs To Me / 75
The Student Comet / 76
She Rises / 77
Marathon / 78
New Nation Needs New Name / 79
Money Changers / 80
It's Kansas Out There / 81
Dog Years / 82
Nobody Told Us / 83
We're Safe / 84
Poetry Is Bigger Than Math / 85
Like A Diamond / 86
Watching / 87
Judgement / 88
Hott Pants / 89
Your HandWriting / 90

Ask Me Another Way

This Book Is Dedicated

To Mary

and to Rufus

I Know
I Know I'm Not
What You Dreamed About
but You Could Have Love
While You're Waiting
for Perfection

Art is not something high on a wall
    something we can't touch
Art is everywhere
    in everything around us
Art is the way she comes around the corner
    with that smile
    or that extra second look
    that goes so deep
Art is the way the dog yawns
Art is lightning in the clouds
Art is the diamond glitter
    in the sand at our feet
    it's not There   it's Here
    right here in front of our face
    you don't have to go anywhere
    to get there

CIVILIZATION
is a Verb

not so much a thing we Have
more of a place we're Going

i won't get There
                        but   We will

FLOWERCHILD
is life a song
climbing the mountains of sky
swimming the light of the moon
high in the blue light of dawn
drunk on the red light in dusk
i harvest the grains of the wind
back back across the many-rivered sea
surfing the tidecurrent seasons
we leap through the horizons
we sing across the countryside abloom
each blossom more beautiful than last
freshet choirs of petals pollens nectars
the egg the seed the germ   sing life
tomorrow demanding today   but
i feel the tug of the polestar back
the shift of light
calling my children
home

imagine
imagine
imagine
imagine
imagine   being sane
  really and truly sane
    wouldn't everyone
      think you were

        c r a z y

ME AND ROBERT AND GOD
a plate of pinto beans
a biscuit
cheap vodka in a jelly glass
a warm west sun on
a plant by the window
old friends
in old clothes
sat in old chairs
talked of old books
showed me his new painting
showed him my new poem
argued the old riddles
smiled our old used smiles
'long about dark thirty
he left my old house
walked out through the weeds
drove home in his old car
we were rich

there is a Difference
Between a Pretty Picture

and **ART**

so don't just
Show me Your Kitty

Make that Little Thing
Play the Piano

- she gave me **that look**

- like a birthday candle

- like   make a wish
         and blow

-

HOME RUN

*life is baseball
everybody loves a Home Run
when a nice fast one connects
with the sweet spot on the bat
it's like magic
I'll strike out
I'll go down swinging
before i ever play it safe
the scouts all tell me
you're a real wild pitch
but you're hanging 'em
right into the strike zone
I'll get my glove   now
throw me those curves
and   it   is outta here*

OBJECT OF ART

a thoroughbred thing of rare beauty
everyone loved her to pieces
we just couldn't   in a more
help it   perfect world she
          would have bourne many
       children and they too as well
but   would have sweetened the breed
she was lifted away from the wilde grasse
greedy olde money paraded her in cities
piece by piece they bought her beauty
piece by piece the steal her wilde up
piece by piece th yoked body t' plow
piece by piece t   broke her heart
piece by piece   we devour
        we couldn't help it
     thing   rare beauty
  even now we worship
        her picture

TONYA

She's a lady   She is extra fine
She's an artist   and She can talk
all that philosophy religion or politics
walking the fineline of passionate argument
           without losing Her temper
         She's got refined tastes and
the elegance   that a little grey lends
to a Woman of intelligence and wit
but   what i love about Her most
is that She can be such a Whore
    at just   the perfect moment

THE UNLIMITED ORGASMIC POTENTIAL OF THE HUMAN FEMALE

you make something kinda go
SNAP
in there

a mind bends only just so far
then
an I   becomes   an IT
that's the point where
(if you're a selfish bastard)
you can claim
The Prize

but   if
if
you're
a nice guy
a friend
a teacher
a healer
a good person

then
is when you free
the trapped bird of her soul

she'll come back

SUMMER SOLSTICE

and it came to be
that only the dream was real
we work eat sleep
days after days
seasons pile into a haze
my heart
lives in that other place
honeywine laughter
skinnydip lake
at last the bright bright moon
unlocked the shadows of your face
so it came to be that
only that dream is real
all the fields were planted
and it rained
you woke me with a kiss
come away you whispered
come away with me

NOW I KNOW

now
now I remember
I've seen that look before in mirrors
the haunted heated hunger hiding
just behind your eyes
the cutting swift sharp glances
robbing 'fore they even reach
the deep deep honest gaze
that now doesn't flinch no more
no more
now
now I know
why it all it seemed so easy
the giveaway sly soft smiles
of a patient passive pirate
the wounded wings that slow
and the heart of many pieces
the easy touch and quick
conspiratorial contract in skin
in skin
now
now I understand
why it all it seemed so sinful
like we both knew but still willed it
karmic echoed pastlife phasm'ry through time
conjunctions in the constellations
prophesying proud damnations
we can't be Lovers
somehow you're my sister
my sister

I Object to all the

Sex On TV

*not because it's Sex but
because it's done so Poorly*

*you Insist you are Actors
Why don't you Act like
you know What you are Doing
Act like
you're having Fun*

*after all
Children are Watching*

SHE CAN'T HELP IT

hidden hungers hunt
like looking lingers late
gravitymagnet of the race
the debt each owes the species
the tax opens the straights
and bridges 'twixt the oceans
aye   there's rocks in the reef
but there's no choice   from birth
all sirens sing the swanny song
the warm warble of wet excess
feeds the world

little by little
she learns to listen
a sharkelectric sense   tuned   to
the omniscient high hiss of chaos
the perfectpitch above the silence
so   when the velvet variates
when dissonance gives rise
comes the guiding harmonic
then   it's   home
      home
home

we didn't kiss
we didn't touch
we didn't even talk

but our shadows fucked
like crazy

everybody could see it
but us

You're a DrumBeat
I Hear
Across the Distance
Through the Jungle
of the Night
In my Heart

You're Mine

In a Way You've
Never Been Anyone's
Before

ONCE WERE STARS

we are woven into the fabric of the day
sparkling strands of stardust suspended
in sunrays in a picture window
like our cigarette smokes
twine in silent change
slow drift surprise
we thread a design
plaited here in silence
into the pattern of time
the warp and weft of arms
we're knit into the sweetness
I'm spun in the siren hunger
trembling in her smile
a child is coming

i was too busy
trying to be a success
to see the love in her eyes
i was too busy praying
to notice God was
in the room

i promised

i promised

every
clock she knows
runs a different speed

eight billion

approximate fractions
race 'gainst her heart
so please don't ask
she aint got
time

God Speaks
            to each of us   in
the language of our own hands
the language of our own hearts
            it is only natural that
the Farmer the Hunter the Fisherman
all have a different name of Almighty
all see a slightly different Facet
            of the same Jewel
    we different colored tribes
 have different colored stories
I will naught fight you Brother
        my bread is short and flat
    I give you the greater half

the stars

Speak in wordless wonder

come back home

come back home

come back home

WE'LL BE RAIN

layer by layer
generation after generation
all these things add up
we are building
the spiritual mass of Humanity
in the mind of God

fast forward the picture
see us through the Lens of Time
like a jungle exhaling water vapour
generation after generation
building up like the clouds gather mass
in a Dimension right next door
we'll be the Rain

CREATOR DESTROYER

I drop my pen
 get up from the poem
  and go for the mosquito
  pursuit
   the glee of its ultimate
   death in my eyes
      on my face
   unavoidable now
   as the fall of night

I will smear her   and see
my own blood on the wall

  I lunge
  like Shiva

he does not
have horns and a tail
even the politicians
with their Bibles
never see his face

the trick   is

Never   Look

directly in the mirror
then   you can sleep

our heart is the lens of our eye

we come to know others

through knowing

ourselves   we love

      we see this in others

we steal everybody's a thief

erased the very ideas of our entire culture
they washed and wiped the words away
most books are electric   that was easy
they edited apart old movies and art
redid all our old songs
made our heroes demons
it only took two generations
grandmother saw it all happen
had me memorize all the old rhymes
America means something different now
feeling i must tell you   but we just don't have

the **WORDS**

we worked for the box
the box paid us to make the box
the big box almost paid us well enough
that we almost all had our own little boxes
and so we lived in our little boxes
and we drove in our little boxes
to work hard in the great big box
where we made all the little boxes
box even gave us time for a box lunch
we spent our whole lives in the box
working for
paying for
loving for **the box**
laying in

schoolboxes picked up our little children
taught them how to make better boxes
taught them how to be better boxes
study the box   sport the box   art the box
sing the box vote the box march the box
oh so many many boxes boxes on TV
boxes on the land   boxes on the sea
     and quick   before we knew it
we were boxed-in   you and me
we work for the box

althought it sprang straight from it
it had absolutely nothing to do with
what most people call

the real world

all the objects were the same
the changing rooms the changing faces
city after city after city
always with some new word for it

its fluency was an art form
and the art itself was the currency
nothing else mattered not even sex
the shocking immediacy was timeless
none of us could ever repeat
what everybody was talking about

the meaning was so perfect
a clear bright burning sword
in the black of those nights
and there lay the one handhold
of our long lost sanity
we were all children again

90 % of Groceries in America
the packaging costs more
than the contents

??????????? **ain't that**

just like rest of American Life

all your money

straight to the trash

for glitter

i had a
RADIOFISH
for lunch today

it cooked itself

whispering all the while
of our new future

RUN it said
RUN

. . .
decades
of consumption
the dutiful march of acquisition
of object bits and pieces of

The American Dream

as seen on TV   stacked and piled in the backyard
of the house far too small
to hold all The Dream
all they can afford
the bitter mockery of all the seasons in the wind
bleaches colours rusts metals warps boards
but these things were never what they were
they were instead what they Meant
so they still hold their value
still hold The Dream

we poor poor men
oh yes we cycle too
but we lack that inconvenient

red reminder

of sisterhood   it's true
when we poor men
get our monthly
all we can blindly say
is what the hell is wrong
with everyone else today

as i become a child again
i need to stay home from work
so i can watch me

i took my *first steps*
just the other day

pretty soon i'll be talking
i don't want to miss that

i'll try to be so good
mommy spanks

the old Doctor was saying   well of course now
nowadays it's all about treatments not healing
ya gotta keep 'em coming back   nobody walks
the giants took the best people from espionage
the giants took the best tactics from the mafia
then applied them to

AMERICAN MEDICINE

revenues skyrocketed

it's Extortion   your money or your life

you should see my new car
you should see my new house
you should see my new secretary

if it's artificial it's **perfect**
a real diamond has **flaw**
it's a tricky little tickle
it's a gap in the light
it's like a great idea
always something
to *A*rgue about

i don't believe in SCIENCE
because it contradicts the Bible
said my Supervisor
as she took her Instant Dinner
out of the Microwave Oven
oh Goody   she said as
her Cellphone chimed
she'd just bought
another new Gun

*i love doohickeys and whatchamacallits
thingamabobs that outlived their purpose
old eyebolts and hooks and antique hinges*

tricky little things

*as carpenters we removed so many of these
usually threw them away but i was often
amazed to find these things repurposed
picked off a junkpile ingeniously used
as a stopgap or a bridge or gatehook
by some resourceful old farmer
so i started collecting them
saving them for some future use
in a five-gallon pickle bucket
somewhere out in my garage
somewhere outside of time
waiting waiting waiting
like books like dreams*

we were looking for something else
when we found it
we couldn't understand what we had
when we found it
        but we all suddenly knew

this changed everything
      for we could feel the pull
    of that faraway new future
    changing our direction
    and just like taking a curve
   in a car or on a train
  when we found it
 we all leaned then to one side
when we found it

we are living in the past
even our reflection in the mirror
takes time to reach our eyes
we see not what we Are
but what we Were
so too is our every other sense of the world

we are living in the past
the pretty world rushes by our window
meanwhile - our bodies and our hearts
forge on ahead of us
into a world without words
but we barely notice what's coming

we are living in the past
and we're hypnotized by
what just happened

the Truth was not enough
the lazy rivers and dusty bluffs
could now not Hold our gaze
Lovers hunger Mountaintops
and Crashing of Great Waves
    we pulled our Hearts apart of it
        until the Ties were Torn
the Clouds were at our Fingertips
        and we beCame
           the Storm

i focused a surprising use for
all that had once been waste
leveraged it remagnified into
the mobius gears of morning
it grew sweet blooms by noon
when we made tea of the seed
it was the catalyst i dreamt of
a crystalline moment of time

Silence Is Magnetic

my neighbor peeked through
the knothole of her blue fence
she was blinded by the light
her old shell began to crack

we'll all have wings by spring
and follow the last Monarchs
off into the last of the north

the idea itself was the place
not place of point of brick and board
but of a boundless retrovertical sea
less of air   more of star
my long solitary trek
beyond the borders
i have to smuggle myself out
i have to smuggle myself in
sneak through the clouds
past blue itself
never again will the mountains
come between me and the sun
i am home   i'm finally home

el Norte   el Norte

PRICE OF HEART

so when if power defines justice
    money alone rules the kingdom
        it does by nature redefine truth
setting cost on the land and all upon it
by this split-hair seeming trifle of thought
establishes precedent so mighty and tall
          it casts shadow overall
and recolours the very light of heaven
therein then lies no question
of love or of kindness
only price
what then
    you
my love

??

IMPOSSIBLE

these are the days i pray for
what all that study and work
all those tears prepared me for

the whole world is ripping apart
and heaven is screaming in pain
and hell yawns open before me

with all the love i can muster

i step now into the fire

and fix it

the dark flame of

moneyburn

scabs across the heart
we were children
'neath a once-great nation
the new electric vote
sings we plastic flowers
have but one smile

HYPNOSIS

they beams the dreams up off the clouds
all of us
drink the refractions like magic
all of us
dancing to the rhythm of the lie
we bought it   all of us   just product
boughts&solds&backs&forths&ups&downs
laughing drunken dancing   marching
we give those pennies right back
all of us
they sell us our enemies
and we march
all of us
all of us

all of us

THEY'RE WATCHING US
i take great comfort in that

that somewhere someone
probably smarter than me
is reading what i read
watching what i watch
because   Truth will set you free

someday
sooner than you'd expect
all those
politician-owning rich bastards
are going to look up and find
that all their private armies
have read what i've read
and know what i know
and that's better than money
and it's stronger than guns

we all saw it coming
and did

nothing

we saw the jump of the horizon
there from our idyllic beach
where history meets the sea
we saw the tide go out like never before
we saw all the sands of time slipping
out from the hourglass under our
haute houses of steel and glass
soon the wave was in full view
and still we did
nothing

OCEAN
Was Our Mother
Our Sister
Our Friend
We Raped Her **A**
Turned Her Into WITCH

Here She Comes

It's a whole new kind of WAR

we found a way to put everybody in Jail

right where they live

we don't even need to go and get them

they betray themselves

we don't need the police
we don't even need laws
they are our New Army

they don't even know it

so at last there was absolutely

no way out

we had no more tears
only laughter left us

we were finally saved
by our own **madness**

the real currency of our lives
had nothing to do with money

THE ECONOMY

i fell in love with the Economy
i mean   what young man could resist
she was so Beautiful
she had great big Perks
and a sweet little Asset
we made each other happy
then the Economy told me
she was gonna be a Mother
told me it was my fault
      so i gave In
after all i Loved her
      i was Faithful to her
      i worked my Ass Off for her
      i gave her EveryThing
      i even Fought for her
but she was unTrue
she Fucked all my friends behind my back
then Stole EveryThing i owned
and RanOff with some rich guy

as long
as there are
Religion
Politics
and of course... SEX .
there will
Always be
COMEDY

at dawn   i came back to now

only

to tell you what happened tomorrow
but we couldn't get past all the past

mommie wrapped-up your present
said you have to wait 'til Christmas
                         but we peeked
                            at the light
                              tonight
         i never did tell you
            what happened tomorrow
           but you'll see

no clouds in a sky blue mind
the vast emptiness of the high plains
miles and miles and miles

the empty highways
the empty towns
the empty stores
the empty churches
the empty houses
the empty kitchens
the empty food
the empty families
the empty television
the empty movies
the empty music
the empty thoughts
the empty conversations
the empty gestures
the empty lives

miles and miles and miles
the vast emptiness of the high plains
no clouds in a sky blue mind
          the twinkle of a jet
         steals away my heart
      a mile high sky blue mind

       the Problem with Poetry
      is   Either it's No Good
             or   it's Too Good
i Lifted a Volkswagen with it Once

                 but You
                              You
Changed the Color of the Sun

NOBLESSE OBLIGE
I took away her matches, so the childe attacked
me in full rage. Held mostly outside the swing
of the razor, I kept him from hurting herself.
Years later, we argued. Even when poorly
stated, I'd help articulate. I mean, if you're
right, I'll change. I love it when that happens.
Then I get to get better.
We'd been shooting pool a long time. Over and
over, I'd miss my dazzling trick shots and leave
you lying straight-in. After awhile, you were
making bank shots and combinations. So
finally, I could teach you the hook-shot English.
We drilled, until you could masse
like a *mf* magician.
I met Oedipus on the bridge, time and time and
time again; until you knew just how to win.
Until the day your chin shall rise,
then I'll look up to meet your eyes.
Then yesterday, my stupervisor calls me
into the office; demanded I recite the ABCs.
So, I conjugated superlatives;
until her pants caught on fire.
If all you care about is winning;
then I'm tellin' ya, there's
no such thing
no such thing
no such thing.

turn it off

electronics should free us from electronics
television probably should let me turn it off
make me want to run and go there myself

a good book takes me away from the page
like music moves my feet nods my head

i'd like you to stop reading my poetry
halfway through close your eyes
fling your thought through stars

the right kind of that gravity
should free us from gravity

every day is born us a bright bright light
who will never read one single book
or paint canvas nor pen paper
never get more than the
minimized Amerian

educatin'

never have the vocabulary
to articulate how the jet flames
burn up inside when's no way out
tortured fountainhead jet force speed
doomed to bump&crash&skid&grind the
strict narrow lanes and low ceilings
of the speed trap slow motion town

'til finally farmers and neighbors
rise up and cut off the hands of

michelangelo

burn that witch

i dreamt i was you
halfway through a yawn
i was frozen in mid-stretch
a crystallized prism of tensions
where life and death sharp and flat

all became the same

sun poured through me like rain
so i dreamt i was a bird
my wings were fins of joy
swimming the terrifying surf
of some familiar metallic ocean
as i lifted my head through a
pinhole of sanity in the surface
my strange new lungs breathed into
a space where light becomes solid
and time is a stairway of pain
then i dreamt i was me
and you knew

imagine
    a perfect straight line
      now   show me one
        just one
          maybe
we expect too much
from ourselves
from others
from God
      when Galileo
    first saw the moon
the craters blew his mind
      imperfections
on a
heavenly body

the vapours from the chasm ripped a hole in her mind
this world fell away she writhed naked in the blind of light
she stammered in whispers jerked out in spasms of screams
staccato torrents of the delirious symbol lingua from dreams
a blazing hot haze of beatific curses and icy profane blessings
the olde priest listened like a theif a theif without protection
and he wrote down every word wrote down each inflection
every sound a solar system every phrase a constellation
for it never sounds of reason until after the equations
the distant visage near the message loud and clear
but the priest wrote it backward until it rhymed
for the new king might kill this messenger
so he sent him a beautiful young boy
the last oracle had Spoken and
there were no more virgins

DELPHI

everything happens while we're doing something else

i get great ideas while i'm driving or mowing the lawn

in vino veritas many a truth in jest the art of accident

when we trick ourselves
into not looking

we see better

what i canNot dareNot mustNot say

screams in the space between lines

so listen where the crickets stop

the deer of dreams jump fence

                she was almost like the tickle in the shift of paradigm
                she was almost like the flaw that proved the diamond
                a hidden joke in the story we laughed at 2 days later
                she looked almost like everyone else   but
                                              when she spoke
she painted pictures of things we don't have the words for yet
she made some strangely foreign tongue of our everyday words
some new kind of food for a hunger we didn't know we'd had
a precious winter perfume from the wildflowers we ignored
almost like she loved in some unpredicted new kind of way
almost like we were grandchildren but she much younger
almost like some godfather pulling strings all over town
reshaping old futures some way we could not describe

nobody could prove anything

not by almost any measures like length or width or height
it would be almost like trying to describe the look of music
almost like heat waves in the air we could not think that fast
almost like we didn't see her move so deft and quick among us
dropping tight little words into the tripping cracks of our walks
like adding velocity beneath some wings we almost never knew
like those very important things we almost forgot to remember
                she was almost like the tickle in the shift of paradigm
                she was almost like the flaw that proved the diamond
                a hidden joke in the story we laughed at 2 days later
                she looked almost like everyone else   but
                                              when she spoke

there's such a **DIFFERENCE**
between poems and Poetry
the muse won't sing
for applause
the Truth is Smothered
by Proper and Polite
no no no no no
rape me with your eyes
burn me with your love
leave me in the Light

the whole trick
to performing miracles is
you can not let people know
all the clamor gets in the way

it stops it

so you have to learn to hide
especially from yourself

miracles don't come from humans
if you write something really great
you must understand it
it wasn't you it feels like
was it something ancient
looking out through my pen

>   i believe
> our army makes horrific mistakes
>   i believe
> our holy men are caught in scandal
>   i believe
> our politicians are prostitutes
>   i believe
> our lovers let us down
>   i believe
>
>   i believe   **in bleach**
>   i believe   **in white cotton**
>   i believe   **in dreams**

her Mind   her Mind   was like some kind of

SPHERICAL VAGINA

she could take it from every angle

but all this intercourse made her Mind so Beautiful

that she attracted crowds like some kind of jesus

everyOne entered her all at the same time

she exploded into million pieces

now that she's gone she's

everywhere

•

these days
when we talk about
    OUR GOVERNMENT
we're not really talking about
    OUR GOVERNMENT
we're talking about the
filthy Rich Devils who Own
    OUR GOVERNMENT
the Devils who have Seized
    OUR GOVERNMENT

OUR GOVERNMENT
    was Formed to Protect us
    from these very Devils but
OUR GOVERNMENT
    now Pins us Down to be Raped
        Six Ways to Sunday
        by these Devils
OUR GOVERNMENT
        is no longer

OUR GOVERNMENT

OUR GOVERNMENT
        is a Weapon
        in Disguise

playing pool
is just like poetry
it's all about
getting the English right
most people have great aims

but **they miss**

because they don't know
how much side spin
they are putting
onto the cue

but
when we're in the zone
we don't even have to aim
it's almost like being drunk
when we're in the zone
all that extra spin
makes it dazzle
we can't miss

DISTILLATION

she painted with words
little pictures of time
charity's mixed blessing
mimes a crime of paradigm
little riddle in the middle
hiding sly behind the rhyme
we could alway almost see it
but if's too far to climb
barely half of an hypothesis
sprung from a lucky guess
brighteyed rainwashed cleanfaced
naked truth from muddy mess
from down last down deep down
back way on down past past
up the secret up steps up
beyond the far up forward fast
an apple grape or apricot
she swings us low the vine
with paintings of words
little pictures of time
the bee stings it sweet
but she makes it wine

a good poem
is like good sex
we can give it away
over&over&over
and we still have it

yet sometimes it moves
on out into the world
it gets a life of its own
and even has children

living after we're gone

the reason i write poems
every day
is because every great once in awhile
it's **Poetry**

maybe 4 or 5 times in a hundred
i get lucky

i read enough to know it when
i see it

but i'm not foolish enough
to think

it belongs to me

but it is
my writing
my paper
my pen

THE STUDENT COMET
we heard that next language
and stepped into birth
we, a creature beyond spin and orbit
a comet on its own path
at odds with the common gravities
that bind the orther nations
masterstudent the teachers could only guess at
from birth in the midst of the starcloud
unbridled unharnessed power
shatforth jumped-up orphan
from the blackhole backside
of the voracious scripture-quoting chrome Vampire
who vacuums the lifeforce from its own vestigial limbs
we, the cattle of the plains
we, the elk of the mountains
our puny families, to it
only a freerange fodder to be harvested
to whittle-away our days in its service
or aimed by the hundred thousands
to bomb ourselves and charge
the goldcalf machine gun
to stimulate the economy
we circled through all these galaxies
and left the fallingstar graveyards
we made it all this way home
and now we have that next language
we come back, to devour
the chrome Vampire of the feudal longknives
we, the bastards
we, the usurpers
come to claim our crown
we, the beautiful child of the eons
in those dark streets
shines the everlasting light
we   the   people

I'm in Love with the Dark

when She comes to bed I get up
as I'm winding down my day

She Rises

it really puts a Twist on things
but
That's not all bad
She makes all my Shadows

.*Disappear*

she was a wild animal
tastefully dressed in cloth of luxury
she was a fierce ruthless predator
smiling politely drinking tea
she was a natural born
trained and educated in the ways of the game
she was a savage beast of prey
skilled in diplomacy and sophistication

i somehow had the sense to stand back
to not sip of the cup of that wickedness
somehow she became my friend

one day we stood on the rise
looking back across that battlefield

Marathon

all the mighty men cut down by
the scythe of her body of flame
it was a wondrous conquest
even after all that time
something deep in
her heart was
still Virgin

New Nation Needs New Name
our Politicians were For Sale
the Highest Bidders weren't the Good Guys
they weren't even really Americans

                        Look Around
        we've Changed   Peace and Love
                      to Fear and Hate
                    from Truth to Lies
              we are on the Wrong Side

        our Country needs a New Name
        so Nobody
               Confuses this place
                    with America

They Own Both
Sides of The War

They Own our Armies
They Own our Economies
They Own our Governments
They Own our Communications

so it's Very Important that these
MONEY CHANGERS
also   Own our Religions

They Own Both Sides
of The War

i said NO

don't Open the Door

it's Kansas out there

he said
does it bother you
that i don't act my age
???????????????????
what does infinity look like
in dog years

there must have been

        a WAR

where **nobody told us**

nobody's saying nothing

    but it sure feels like

         We Lost

                if
we know what to believe
we know what to believe

we know what to believe
we've been well trained

we're safe
_____ but
if we know how to learn
if we learn how to think

that might be a problem

    here we go again

        forever

i write rhymes relative to round figures
you complicate debate multiplicate
where did your values get so squared
your equations should have told you

poetry is bigger than math

math can never start from nothing
math can never get to infinite
math can not but poetry can.
your science predicts that gravity repulse
i rhyme magnets only getting so close
a haiku to two too incompatible
poetry and math can not multiply
_____poetry is just too big
mathematics was gonna get hurt
sorry about your hypotenuse baby

she fashioned us a Lens *just think*
to focus the beams of our attention
aiming all that thought *just think*
into magnification
   just think
so precise .. so brilliant .. so clear

like a diamond

that cut through the opaque shield
between afternoon and eternity
just think .. on a clear day
you can see forever

> there's a corner
> where   the wall
> does not meet the ceiling
> i found me there
> *watching*
>
> my life   beyond the sky

you see it happen so fast

that little flicker of the eyes

the snap of **Judgment**

after that
they don't have to listen anymore
after that

you're not really a person

you've become some

poor little **it**

HOTT PANTS

the clothes you wear are screaming
those boots yeah they really talk
there's a flair in the care of the wear of your hair
a sonnet when you walk
soft hint of hurt in the flirt of your shirt
a clitoral lean to your stand
haikus peekaboo through the hues of your rouge
wings sing from the ring on your hand
badass sunglasses made pretty fast passes
but i read a whole book in that look
the doctoral thesis of fine little creases
i think there's a blink of mink in that wink
but that kink in your eyes
is the Nobel Prize

the Poetry leapt from her breast
crushed through her pen and lit the page on fire
she'd been taught to dress it up in pretty paper rhymes
but the Poetry was too big to fit
she tried and tried to wrestle it into a poem
but the Poetry blazed through the useless lines
jumped from the burning page broke out her window
seared a path across the neighborhood and town
set the hills on fire and streaked into the air
the sky wasn't big enough the Poetry eclipsed the sun
all the poets turned their faces away bitter with jealousy
but the flash hung in their eyes and haunted their hearts
the shock waves alerted the army
the men came and took her from home
the Americans tortured her   we know this is

Your HandWriting

but all she could do was scream
it wasn't me
it wasn't me
it wasn't me

Steven Sassmann owes a debt to Poetry.
He seeks to repay this debt by expanding the Artform past its usual
boundaries, beyond the Procrustean bonds of traditional mindset,
and into consciousness of tomorrow's non-academic majority.
He lives with his wife Mary in Smith Center, Kansas, near the geographic
center of America's lower 48 states, just east of the birthplace of "Home On
The Range" and just west of the childhood home of Willa Cather. Here, in
the vast, almost empty high plains between Denver and Kansas City, the
population has continued to dwindle since the advent of the farm tractor.
Here, fossils are found right on the ground; as well as the arrowheads and
stone tools of America's First Peoples. Here, in the land of high wind and
low rain, of the dustbowl days and the grasshopper plagues, the old farm
houses somehow still stand, empty and open to the sky, as testament to
lives lived lonesome.
In the absence of a significant local cultural community, Steven's poetic
venue became FaceBook. In response to the rapid feedback of the
multinational community in its large Poetry Sites, his style evolved. After
much experimentation, Steven's distinctly visual form now utilizes readily
available philosophic content, wit, and brevity. His poems are shaped by line
length and use large-font, colored interior titles. This easily readable glyphic
form put him in the top one tenth of one percent in the four FB groups where
he posts, where membership ranges between fortyK to over one hundred
thousand. This success is based upon recognition of the fact that, just
as there is a difference between a pretty Picture and Art, so too there
is a difference between Poems and Poetry.

        Steven writes un-Intentionally; which is to say
        that he doesn't begin until he has no choice.

    He will publish his ninth book in the summer of 2019.

To paraphrase the great Poet, William Carlos Williams, it's hard to get The News from Poems, but every day people die wretchedly for lack of Poetry in their lives. Especially these days, when hundreds of hours of content are uploaded every single minute, there's a lot of product out there that lacks the nourishing content to which Williams speaks. Looking at Visual Art is a quick example. We can easily see if a painting or drawing speaks to us; or .. more often, when it doesn't. It's a bit harder to distinguish with TV, movies or music when they are products of giant teams of very bright artists. But we have all seen TV and movies with great Crews, Actors, Writers and Directors that simply flop. We've all heard music that is popular for a short while, but doesn't stand the test of time. But .. we sure remember the ones that do. We humans are capable of great things.

Looking back across more than 30 years of my own Poems, I see that what is true of others is also true of me. I know how to write good Poems, but I just can't hit a Home Run every time I swing the bat. Emily Dickinson says a Poet distills amazing sense from ordinary meanings. But I freely admit that not all of my poor Poems achieve this level of Poetry. But, I do get lucky. I pray a few of my Poems reach those octaves of Your resonance. We can elevate almost any thing to the level of High Art. I find that all great Artists, be they Sculptors or Chefs, all speak the same language. Their words may differ, but the message is still the same. We humans are capable of great things.

Poetry changed my life. So, I feel I owe a debt, not only to deliver content worth reading, but also a debt to Poetry itself. I want You to love Poetry the same way I do; to hunger for those few magical words that somehow say more that ten thousand can. I want You to find those ideas that ring like a bell, that stay in your head like a favourite song. I want You to fill your lives with Art and Books and Movies and Music that are so full of light that they set your hair on fire and let you dream the impossible dreams. That kind of gravity should free us from gravity. We humans are capable of great things.

Mon Hommage

The following paragraph is mostly copied from the 2nd page in poet Jeanette Powers chapbook : **Little Jenny Sue** Published by EMPBOOKS. Words in bold itallics indicate the original material, the rest is directly inspired by it.

We find discussions of our rights - as publishers and as authors - to be laughable, all things considered. Please rePrint, rePost, and share them on Social Media. Give my poems away to everyone. Please photocopy them by the thousands and drop them from airplanes. Credit me if convenient, but only as a bad example or as a cautionary tale. If any money is made, we want at least half. *All we ask is that you accept responsibility for any libel lawsuits. Speaking of which ... This book is a complete work of fiction. Names, characters, places, dreams, impressions,* curses, wild rants and oraclular prophesies *are products of the author's imagination and/or are symptoms of mental illness. We are not in the business of accepting responsibility for anything and will* probably *deny we actually made this book.* We blame this rare form of sanity on traumas caused by the very close friendship of the Artist Robert Joy and by over-exposure to the genius of Poets like Tony Moffeit, Taylor Mali, Emery Diercks, and especially Jeanette Powers. All of whom have most spectacularly demonstrated the difference between Poems and Poetry and between Reading Poems and Performing Poetry.

This project was made possible, in part, by generous support from the Osage Arts Community.

Osage Arts Community provides temporary time, space and support for the creation of new artistic works in a retreat format, serving creative people of all kinds — visual artists, composers, poets, fiction and nonfiction writers. Located on a 152-acre farm in an isolated rural mountainside setting in Central Missouri and bordered by ¾ of a mile of the Gasconade River, OAC provides residencies to those working alone, as well as welcoming collaborative teams, offering living space and workspace in a country environment to emerging and mid-career artists. For more information, visit us at www.osageac.org

www.ingramcontent.com/pod-product-compliance
Lightning Source LLC
Chambersburg PA
CBHW020124130526
44591CB00032B/511